I P⟨ Your Stocking

Good World War

If you found this book it means that I pooped in your stocking. In the proceeding pages you will find out why I pooped in your stocking and why you deserved to be pooped on. If you take this poop to serious then poo poo to you.

With All My Poop

Poop Master P

Table Of Contents:

The top 10 reasons why you found poop in your stocking. Counting down to the best reason at 10.

1. You spend a lot of time in the bathroom. It makes people think you have a poop obsession.

2. Sometimes the words that come out of your mouth make you seem like you have poop in your teeth.

3. Your pet dog got carried away this year and left you a home made present.

4. Your family has a good sense of humor and decided this year instead of candy they wanted to give you poop in your stocking.

5. Now you can brag to everyone if they ask that you got poop in your stocking.

6. There was a coal shortage for bad kids and well this was the best alternative.

7. The Christmas tree you cut down or bought this year wanted to have one last hurray before it completely dried up and was turned into kindling. Poop Tree Style.

8. You spend to much time playing video games so your avatar character jumped out of the television set and let poop in your stocking.

9. Santa couldn't get into the bathroom this year and found the best place to hide the evidence.

10. You poop so much that you actually left poop in your own stocking.

A Poop In Your Stocking Poem To Spread Christmas Cheer

There is poop
There is poop
There is poop in my stocking
What did I do
To deserve this loving.
Was it Santa,
Was it reindeer,
Or was it my Dad.
Did I sleep walk last night
Because I had to go real bed.
Cus there is poop
There is poop
There is poop in my stocking
I think I go cry, wash my hands,
and start yelling.

Different ways to say Poop from Around the World, Educate yourself.

America - Poop
China - poop
Russia - poop
France - poop
Japan - poop
Thailand - poop
Greece - poop
Phillipines - poop
Dutch - poop
Australia - poop
Navajo - poop
Swedish - poop
Danish - poop

You say poop the same no matter what language since its an english word.

Top 10 Fun Ways To Say You Have To Poop

1. Time to drop some kids off at the pool.

2. I am going to go make some brown babies.

3. I am tired of playing pick a boo with myself, so I am going to go drop a bomb.

4. Time to make a symphony of brown.

5. Paul Reverie is farting saying the poo are coming the poo are coming.

6. You ever heard of a cleave land steamer, well I am about to take one all over that bathroom.

7. I need to do the wiki wiki oh so very quickly quickly.

8. Poop. Its whats for dinner.

9. I am about to poop so hard that I might go over to the dark side.

10. Call of poopy is my favorite game.

The Poo A Story Of Brown

Once upon a time there was a poo that lived in the woods. He wasn't sure who his mother or who his father was. It was all so very confusing. Then when day he came across a cave where a bear lived. The bear had been sleeping all winter and didn't know that right outside his cave was a poo. In the morning when the bear woke up he sniffed the air. It smelled not so very good. He walked outside and sat down and at that very moment he sat right on the poo.
Now the bears but was all covered in brown.
End…

I know what a poo of a story. Waist of poo time.

Questions about Poo? Can you come up with an answer?

1. Can poo shoot back up inside of you?

2. Has anyone pooped so much that they lost 5 pounds?

3. Can you poop yourself to death?
4. Where can you find the record for worlds largest poop?

5. Has anyone ever clogged a toilet so much with Poo that they had to replace the entire toilet?

6. What was the longest someone has ever gone without pooping?

7. What is the longest someone has continued to consecutively with no breaks been able to poop?

8. Can you make shapes with the poop that comes out of you?

9. Can you have explosive poop cover an entire bathroom wall to ceiling to floor?

10. What does a black color poo mean?

Poop Insults For Online Gaming

I am not sure if you have ever been talked trashed too playing online against someone on a computer or gaming system. I know I have and sometimes the more childish you can go with your trash talking the anger people will get against you, which leads to hilarious replies or messages from them. Here are some of my favorites. Use with caution or in general don't use them at all. They work rather well.

- Oh man I just shot you in the face with a poop and you died.

- I just pooped in your mouth and you liked it.

- I just took a poop all over your bed. Good luck sleeping tonight.

- Poop is whats for dinner.

- I know you like the poop, but you take it in the poop.

- You better take notes because the poop be coming.

- You just got poop stabbed.

- You don't understand that you are just a tiny poop in the universe.

- Your face kind of looks like a poop mixed with peanut butter.

- Sometimes you eat a poop pie, but you just ate an entire poop buffet.

- Squishy squishy, poop all over you.

- An intruder just broke in to your house and pooped all over your cloths.

- Pooping poopy wheelies.

- Are you guilty of life behind poop.

- You just had an unexpected visitor. Check your pants for poop.

- I am the greatest pooper in all the world.

- No one poop better than me.

- I had no idea that my poop would destroy you.

A Personal Story of How I Stepped In Dog Poop

As as child I liked to play outside in the sprinklers in my backyard. I would throw foam noodles back and forth across two sprinklers in my backyard with my brother. It was good times until one day. That fateful day.

I was having a good time throwing foam noodles back and forth across the sprinklers. When suddenly I slipped and landed on my back. When I got up my back was all covered in something brown and black. My brother was laughing his butt off. What happened. Well before we started playing in the sprinklers outside in the grass we usually use a pooper scooper and clean up the yard. Well I had missed one since it was my turn to pick them up that particular day. Now the poop that I slipped in now was all mushy from the water. It was like slipping on a banana peel and now my foot was covered in dog poop and my back was covered in dog poop. This was absolutely disgusting. It still is a horror that haunts me to this day.

The funniest bird poop ever for a second

When I was about 13 years old I was at the beach in San Diego, California when a couple of mormons approached me and my brother to share there religion. We really weren't all that interested, but as they were talking to us a bunch of sea gulls had been circling around the beach. Suddenly one of the men in front of us just had gotten pooped on the shoulder of his shirt and he didn't even notice. I am trying my best not to laugh, my face turning bright red, until I full blown am laughing so hard. This is where Karma came in and bit me in the but. In the middle of my hysterical laughing I felt something warm hit my cheek, my leg, and the very top of my foot. I look down and my foot and leg have white stuff all over it. Warm, liquid. I wipe my face and my hand comes away with the white liquid on my cheek. I had just been pooped on by some seagulls. I freaked out and just started running and screaming for the nearest beach bathroom shower. I washed and washed and washed. I have never been so grossed out before. This literally beat the time I slipped in the sprinkler dog poop or the time I walked into he living room and without realizing stepped barefoot into a pile of dog poop diarrhea that my dog had left on the carpet as a surprise last night. IF any of this had happened to someone else I would have been laughing my butt off. When its you, well its not so funny.

Poop Questions To Ask Friends

Have you ever stepped in poop by accident before? If so tell the story.

What color is your poop normally?

When you eat beats what color is your poop?

Does your poop float or does it sink?

Have you ever eaten corn just to see how long it takes to process through your system and come out as poo? How long did it take? My records is 4 hours.

Do you laugh when you see a horse poop in a parade and then wait in anticipation for someone to step in the horse poop and then get disappointed when someone avoids the poop and incredibly happy when someone steps right in it?

Have you ever lit a cow pie on fire?

Have you ever thrown your own poop at someone pretending to be a monkey?

Do you get explosive diarrhea poop often? See a doctor if you do often!

Have you ever gone on a walk and suddenly it hits you. You really have to go poo, so you go behind some bushes?

Who poops more men or women?

Do you think that there are people that hang out in restrooms hoping someone doesn't flush the toilet, so they can go look and play with some new poop?

Would you rather be held up by a gun or held up by someone that is threatening to have explosive poop at you cus they just ate a bunch or raw chicken? I say a gun. If you get hit with the explosive poop, Id call it a day!

Do you think cow poop is responsible for global warming?

Why is it that people find it okay to pick up dog poop with a plastic baggy in hand, but aren't into picking up human poop with a plastic baggy and hand.

Why is it that people like to sit in recliners that have toilets in them?

Who came up with bed pans?

Have you ever had a poop so large that it is almost a relief afterwards and painful during?

When was the last time you pooped yourself?

Would you eat bat poop?

Also Available From Good World War

The Stupid, Why Did You Take That Selfie Picture and Post It To The Internet? Handbook

By: Good World War